Outside the Box

OUTSIDE THE BOX

A Wind of Change

Pietro BARBARA

Copyright © 2018 by Pietro BARBARA.

Library of Congress Control Number:		2018903897
ISBN:	Hardcover	978-1-5434-0816-4
	Softcover	978-1-5434-0815-7
	eBook	978-1-5434-0814-0

All rights reserved. No part of this book may be reproduced or transmitted in any form or by any means, electronic or mechanical, including photocopying, recording, or by any information storage and retrieval system, without permission in writing from the copyright owner.

Any people depicted in stock imagery provided by Getty Images are models, and such images are being used for illustrative purposes only. Certain stock imagery © Getty Images.

Print information available on the last page.

Rev. date: 06/11/2018

To order additional copies of this book, contact:
Xlibris
1-800-455-039
www.Xlibris.com.au
Orders@Xlibris.com.au
775341

Contents

Introduction xi
Acknowledgements xv

Chapter 1   Level Playing Field 1
Chapter 2   Energy 6
Chapter 3   Renewing Australian Politics 9
Chapter 4   Climate Change 12
Chapter 5   Indigenous Issues 15
Chapter 6   Australia Day And Independence Day 23
Chapter 7   Superannuation And Retirement 26
Chapter 8   Health Insurance 30
Chapter 9   Employment Ethics 32
Chapter 10 Buying A Home 34
Chapter 11 Education 35
Chapter 12 Respecting Sexual Preferences 38
Chapter 13 Gender Issues 41
Chapter 14 'Me Too' 47
Chapter 15 The Church 50

Chapter 16 Islam Today 52

Chapter 17 Taking Life 55

Chapter 18 Crypto 58

Chapter 19 Religion 60

Chapter 20 Defining Australian 62

Epilogue 65

About The Website 69

About The Author 71

Index 73

Overdue, controversial, game-changing, outside the box concepts that could improve the lives of Australia for many years to come . . . It's time for *change!*

Is this a brave and helpful revelation or just a dream? Only time will tell.

Intentionally brief, and light reading, this work seeks to stimulate, aggravate, and initiate outside-the-box thinking.

You won't agree with everything herein, but if you are thinking about it and considering it, coming up with alternatives, discussing, growling, crying, or laughing instead of knocking and discouraging, you may be outside the box.

I dedicate this work to

Salvino (Sam) Barbara—Bam Bam.

He was a thinker.

Introduction

I was walking through some beautiful untouched native Pilbara bushland near Newman recently, and it struck me that this country deserves a lot better than it's getting in almost every respect. The thought popped into my head, *Poor fellow, my country* (see acknowledgements).

About now you will be saying that this guy sounds like a black fella. Well, wrong again. I'm a white bloke with half a brain. That's according to my dad (bless him), who tested me in many ways. He was a philosopher/cosmologist, educationalist type. My father was about as smooth as a gravel pit and died unrecognised. He wrote books that no one could read. As a devout Catholic, my father even wrote a letter to the pope (before my father died twenty years ago). In a very correct manner, my father suggested to the pope that he had better revisit the whole priest celibacy thing because the clergy are running amok and destroying the church's credibility. He even charged me with sending his letter to each pope (which I have done) in the hope that one of them will wake up. Hmm! The problem, however, was always that his writing was so well done, complex, lengthy, and complete that you need to be a Rhodes scholar with a cut lunch to get to the end of a sentence. I remember him spending days on a single page.

That's why I have adopted what I call a round-the-campfire tone.

So keep going. I've got a bit to say. I may even be right about a few things. See what you think. This is *outside-the-box* thinking. Try it.

I'll do a chapter on the church later, but for now, turn the page, because about now is when I share with you some outside-the-box thoughts on many different topics.

It is most unlikely that all will agree with a lot of what I have to say. That's great because what I am trying to do is to stimulate discussion and hopefully be a catalyst not only for change but improvement, even reform.

This work is a philosophical opinion piece.

- There is no such thing as a wrong opinion.
- There is only my opinion and your opinion.
- It is hoped that this stimulates you to have an opinion.
- The *outside-the-box* banner gives licence to free and creative thinking.

- It creates a safe arena to air and share your thoughts.
- Some will get it wrong, and some won't.
- It's the process we must embrace and encourage.
- Opposing, knocking, and discouraging is common.
- If you disagree, be prepared to say why and come up with something better.
- My favourite saying used to be, 'It is better to remain silent and be thought a fool than to open your mouth and remove all doubt.'

Now I prefer, 'It is better to be heard and to share in the hope that if I got it wrong, you might get it right, than it is to remain silent and blame everyone else

No subject is taboo in the arena of outside-the-box thinking. So please respect each other's right to an opinion, and encourage an environment where, unafraid, all can be heard. I dare say, we can make Australia great.

Acknowledgements

The things that shaped me will perhaps be the subject of another book, but I would like to honour the role Salvino Barbara my father played. He perhaps taught me far too much.

I would like to thank and acknowledge George Eliot for these wonderful words which I have carried close to my heart and quoted many times: *"A friend is one to whom one may pour out the contents of one's heart, chaff and grain together, knowing that gentle hands will take and sift it, keep what is worth keeping, and with a breath of kindness, blow the rest away."*

I would also acknowledge *Poor Fellow My Country*, a book by Xavier Herbert, who 'paints a scene of racial, familial, and political disparity. He lays bare the paradoxes of this wild land, both old and wise, young flawed. Set in the 1930s and Winner of the Miles

Pietro BARBARA

Franklin Award on first publication in 1975, *Poor Fellow, My Country* is masterful storytelling, an epic in the truest sense. This is the decisive story of how Australia threw away her chance of becoming a True Commonwealth. It is undoubtedly Herbert's supreme contribution to Australian literature.'

But with that, it changed nothing and goes unnoticed.

Chapter 1

Level Playing Field

Australia is on the way to becoming a Third World nation. There is no level playing field in a world where some of the players are communist nations with poor human rights records. Third World countries have a workforce that is happy with $40 per day or less. We cannot compete with this. Is the only answer to manufacture nothing and reduce our standard of living with unemployment and stagnant wages till the bar is lower?

Wages, jobs, and living standards have been in rapid decline for at least the last thirty-five years. It's time to wake up. If you want good roads, a healthcare system that works, and everything else we as Australians have come to expect, as well as a job, then you need to pay more than $20 for a wheelbarrow and more than $50 for a chainsaw. Yes, that either means charging a tariff on imported goods or making it a lot easier than it is to manufacture goods in Australia. Personally,

I prefer the latter; but to do either or both, we need to jump out of this ridiculous box we are currently constrained by.

Australia—indeed the world—needs outside-the-box thinking. The populists have in fact realised this. We can see examples around the world of leaders and movements that are pushing the boundaries. Change for change's sake is, however, not what I advocate. Informed, deliberate, calculated, planned change based on outside-the-box thinking is what I advocate.

Australia is one of the few places where almost anyone with money can buy Australian homes, businesses, land, even a port—struth! Have a go at buying even just land in Thailand, Japan, or China and see how it works out for you!

Yes, we are talking radical change. It's about time, I think. And to achieve change, we would need to work together, get outside the box, and forget the quick fix or easy way out. Unfortunately, it's nearly too late. Soon, Australia will be making nothing, all because you cannot have the whole cake as well as eat it all too. We need to be more than a supplier of raw materials. Australians are addicted to buying cheap imported goods but have forgotten that you need a job to pay for them. Like any addiction, the drug addicts are rarely able to make the change. They fear the consequences and pain of cold turkey instead of embracing the victory and empowerment that a change might bring.

Why is everyone obsessed with digging up and virtually giving away what we have as well as allowing every man and his dog to buy what they want? Think about the future and the Australia we leave our kids. Soon nothing will be manufactured in Australia. There is little respect for an Australia that is willing to sell land and business to non-citizens. Australia will even sell a port—anything for short-term political or economic gain, with no thought of the future.

We have leaders who even deny the environmental impacts of their short-sighted policies. We sit by and watch puerile party politics because it has become the norm, and we think we can buy cheap everything without consequence.

The two-party opposition political system, knocking everything and combining with political correctness and the overriding need to get voted back in, has stifled any chance of much-needed, major change. The latest move towards lowering company tax rates is a move in the right direction, but unfortunately, it may again be the wrong move. Why? Because, in the same way, they got superannuation and health wrong. It is the easy way out. It does not consider human nature and greed. It will be abused and, yes, it may help in the short term, but it does not address the fundamental problem of the wealth not being distributed. Further, it does not address the problem of foreign ownership of the corporations who get the advantage of lower company tax as well. We need to encourage 'Australian made and owned' in a way that endeavours to benefit Australians and Australia. Whether it is the government's intention or not, big corporations will employ the best minds in the business to legally minimise or negate their tax burden if they can. It's called *human nature*.

This is certainly outside-the-box. What if the tax were split, with a compulsory small portion paid, perhaps on gross income—and as a minimum. In the normal course of events, this payment would form part standard overall tax, so it should not increase the tax burden for an entity. Of course if the entity was not paying tax—as is often the case—then this proposed tax would be payable. In this way, the country would collect tax first, rather than last or not at all. Currently, many big companies pay very little tax or the country only gets the scraps after every conceivable deduction has been made to legally minimise tax. And why not? It falls within the rules, but as usual does not take into account *human nature*.

Dare I say, put Australia first, then, by all means bring on the proposed company tax rate cuts. At least Australia will get the 3 per cent (or whatever is decided) on gross earnings. It will be more than the *nothing* we currently get.

Then there is the need and problem of distributing the wealth. Once again let's acknowledge the presence of *human nature*. Fundamentally, employers don't want to pay more than they must, workers want as much as the can get regardless of whether the employer can afford it, and businesses would rather spend on capital items and depreciable assets than wages. This is the recipe for conflict that has haunted the world. It is with trepidation that I suggest outside-the-box solutions. Why not make wages more than %100 deductible, with a scale where paying full time employees is more attractive than paying part time and casual? Better still abolish payroll tax, but only for fulltime employees. (a carrot) Or, how about if a minimum wage increase, across the board, could be linked to inflation? (a stick) Even if it were set at half of inflation (as a minimum), I suggest that most workers would be delighted.

The theme that comes through constantly in my thinking is to take the discussion out of basic rights. These rights are no longer optional, and they need to be fair—and importantly they must be *human nature–proof.*

Chapter 2

Energy

We need to think outside the box.

Would a solution that eradicates carbon emissions, complements renewables, and provides cheap or even free power for Australians and Australian industry in an environmentally friendly, sustainable, proven way be of interest? This would help level the playing field and boost manufacturing, living standards, jobs, and more. We would soon be exporting steel and cars instead of just raw materials.

We are a huge geologically stable, scientifically advanced nation with the world's most excellent quality controls, safety standards, and reporting procedures. We are arguably the most regulated society in the world. That makes nuclear power a very viable option for us. It is clean, efficient, and would complement other renewables in a sustainable, reliable, affordable way. I have been a radiation worker for many years. Yes, radiation can be dangerous. But if it's in the right hands, the benefits-to-risk equation is very attractive. It's a tool we know how to use. You don't think twice about having an X-ray. This is because it is performed in a controlled environment by well-equipped, trained personnel who are regulated by a professional body. *Nuclear power* can be the same. Further, Australia is especially suited because we have an abundance of uranium as well as plenty of room to find a place to safe store our own nuclear waste facilities, preferably owned by government, for the benefit of all Australians. This island has a massive coastline to choose from. Facilities cooled by water that, in turn, runs desalination plants, could help relieve water shortages around the country. We could even open new areas that only lack water and power. Hey, there would be so much growth that we would be inviting refuges to come and work in our factories. It is even a green idea. Think about it before you knock it. And if you are knocking it, give me a better suggestion.

If you go to Brunei, you will notice that fuel is very cheap. This is because they have abundance of it. In Australia, the things we have abundance of are cheaper to buy in the countries we export to.

With a radical decrease in energy cost, the price of Australian-made steel, for example, would be a game changer on the world stage. We have the iron ore; we should do more than just dig it up. Oh yes, this could not be done in isolation. It would be in association with other radical, political, and structural change and support. The flow-on would bring an unparalleled era of growth, development of industry, and jobs.

Here are some thoughts that may help level the playing field:

- Facilitate export of frozen and refrigerated Halal meat, rather than livestock export, creating jobs for Australians.
- For Australian primary industry and manufacturing, have a sliding scale of taxes.
- Have 'Made in Australia' rewarded more than 'Assembled Only', with imported products at the other end of the scale.
- Foreign ownership needs to be restricted or controlled as any benefit to Australia will be secondary to their agenda—they will never put Australia first.

This could be addressed in a new constitutional directive on *independence day*. When we declare Australia a republic, perhaps we get to revisit the rules. More on this later.

Next thing you know, Australia will be making cars again, dairy farmers will be back in business, and perhaps entrepreneurial Australians would be encouraged to have a go.

Chapter 3

Renewing Australian Politics

Australia is of age. A good forum for introducing this new way of thinking might be in the context of a new start for Australia. Dare I call it *Independence Day*?

The idea of a republic has been floated before, and there is no better time than now to make changes that redefine Australian values and thinking.

The era of a colonial commonwealth country has passed. We honour and respect the Queen of England. We acknowledge the historical significance the association has brought this country. Further, I think it deeply dishonours her and causes insult to say we will wait till she is dead. Far better, perhaps, to proudly come of age, leave the nest with dignity, and thank the Queen for the part she has played. I suspect we would have her blessing.

The Westminster system of government and our political system are also due for upgrade. A system that encourages and indoctrinates career politicians into an inflexible mindset is not dynamic enough to meet the challenges of the next era. Change, growth, and transformation are what this nation so sorely needs. We will always retain the flavour of the past but need a system able to accept that non-political leaders (who can from time to time) offer revitalisation.

The ways of opposition politics and behaviours exhibited in our parliament, at times, make me ashamed to be Australian. This degrades us on the world stage. It is time for Australia to write an *inclusive constitution* and spell out our values, so defining Australia in a unique way, to include and protect all Australians, for all to see and refer to.

Then there is the flag. Well, if we are going to do this, let's just get it right on day one. A trend developing as we speak is for the showing of two flags. One flag is for indigenous people of Australia, and one is for Australia. Well, this needs to stop. Another way to enrich unity around one purpose and goal is one flag. Yes, there are probably lots of ideas around this, but I suggest that an Australian Republic's independence flag must include—in the least, symbolically—the indigenous flag as well as the Southern Cross and the Union Jack on blue with a central green and yellow map of Australia symbolically overlying yet encompassing all. Perhaps we could even include the kangaroo.

The past is what got us where we are now—the good and the bad. Let's not be shackled by it. If Germany and Japan can look forward, surely Australia can.

Chapter 4

Climate Change

Well, talk about the elephant in the room. This is so obvious that it clearly demonstrates humanity has not yet fully evolved into intelligent, sentient beings that control, respect, and value their planet. There is now an urgent need to address the well-being of our environment.

Economic, political, and social excuses and denial are no longer acceptable. Hard, immediate choices need to be made to slow then halt the process before it is too late. Unfortunately, it seems Australia is sadly lagging on all accounts. Why is this? you ask. The hard truth is that this country is sliding into oblivion, caused by our political system. We have good leaders, but the system does not encourage, or reward, change. There is opposition to every argument. Incumbents are so busy trying not to upset anyone and dodge the knives in the front and back that they are afraid to instigate real change. They would rather take the safe road, upset as few people as possible, be politically correct, and survive another term.

The world should stop burning coal, and Australia needs to stop burning it and exporting it. How puerile we are to think that we can sell coal to Third World countries and think they will burn it efficiently. We barely do these ourselves. Gas is better, if used wisely, but we export our iron ore to countries that produce steel in the cheapest way possible, causing more harm to the environment. Australia has a lot to answer for, on the world stage, as a global contributor to climate change.

The answer again requires outside-the-box thinking, major change, and I dare say it could make Australia great.

If we had abundant affordable power in this country, it would facilitate a new era for Australia. For a start, manufacturing and exporting steel instead of iron ore. Then everything else, including cars.

The only way I can see this happening is with nuclear power. Australia has the resources, infrastructure, technology, and controls to do this properly. I know I have said it before in other chapters of this book, but it is so fundamentally important that it bears saying again.

Nuclear power produces abundant clean energy to complement renewables. Like anything else, if not done properly in the right geologically, politically stable location, there can be serious problems. But done right, in Australia, without cutting any corners and, possibly, government-owned, the advantages are simply staggering. Historically, nuclear power has earned a bad name because of problems caused by poor controls, design, and maintenance, or in the case of Japan, a geologically unstable location. We have the technology and a huge geologically stable land mass. What Australia lacks is vision, national confidence, pride, and the willingness to have a ago.

Chapter 5

Indigenous Issues

The way Australians think of the indigenous folk and the way society and governments consider their needs is, in my view, fundamentally wrong.

From the outset, I must confess that I have had a negative attitude towards our indigenous folk, openly damning, blaming, and ridiculing them. The thought process I am going to introduce you to now was the catalyst for a successful radical change in thinking for me and perhaps can benefit others. Take a big breath of kindness and read on.

Let's pretend for a moment that indigenous folk are members of this 'new' Australian family. Now given it's bloody difficult because their civilization is as older than ours, consider this provoking analogy: *socio-economically, many—even most—of our First Nation people were (and in many cases still are) 'infants'.* Now before you hang me from the nearest tree, please hear me out!

As a cherished adopted member of a family, infants are fed, clothed, housed, accepted, encouraged, nurtured, and educated so they learn to respect themselves, respect others, and finally give and receive love and reach their rightful potential and self-fulfilment. Bloody hell, that was good! I might call it a hierarchy of needs and change my name to start with *M* (Maslow)—ha ha!

Hey, stop laughing! I'm serious.

The Australian family, if you like, 'forcefully adopted' the indigenous people of this land. But they were never really accepted as legitimate family members. Our First Nation people were more like unwanted kids, neither parented well nor loved and valued. And here's the thing: they already had a family and culture that we rejected. (In fact, they were considered less than human in so many ways. There is little wonder that Australia finds itself in the current dilemma.)

Well-parented children, grow and develop normally in a healthy family environment. They will naturally develop to take on the beautiful characteristics of their upbringing, individual nature, and heritage with responsibility and pride. But hang on—that's not what has happened at all to most of the indigenous people of Australia.

A lot of them have grown up now (for many generations actually), and far too many have gone down the wrong road. Yes, we now reap what we have sown!

My kids turned out pretty well, but if I had not been a good dad (as above), they would have ended up just the same, getting into my grog and ruining their lives. Yes, and it would be my fault, not theirs.

Now it must be said that despite this, a lot of our indigenous people have somehow managed to break out of this cycle and become well-balanced, proud individuals. Well, I take my hat off to them. With that, however, I am sure there is a lot of hurt and memories that they could do without.

About now, you'll be thinking, 'It's too late. We can't turn the clock back.' Hmm! Well, we cannot turn the clock back, but it's not too late.

The whole Australian family must be onside. It needs to start with strong leadership. Set the stage. Get the whole mob together, and tell the story with honesty and frank authority that bleeds the truth. Recognise the scars from sins of our fathers so healing can begin.

The key to success is an understanding and universal acceptance of what has happened (see the chapter on education). My analogy of the family and parenting is a valid and useful tool in achieving this first essential step towards softening the many hardened hearts on both sides of the equation.

We cannot expect carnage, cruelty, and broken families to be forgotten. Human history is so full of tragedy that we cannot escape its reality. One thing is clear. Only by moving forward in recognition of the past can better outcomes be achieved. Leave the past behind instead of being shackled by it. There are many examples of this in recent times. Just think on the German story.

Yes, for both sides of the equation, it will involve commitment to change with an understanding that we are all righting a wrong. It may be that we did not personally commit the sin ourselves. We all, however, bear responsibility for its legacy. The first step for non-indigenous Australia is a step towards taking on this responsibility. It will, however, be a waste of time unless the indigenous community take corresponding steps towards forgiveness and acceptance. This two-way softening of hearts is most idealistic, I know; but without it, simply nothing either side of the debate tries to do will ultimately succeed. Payback, bitterness, and division will only enhance the racial divisionary tendency. Clearly, band-aid solutions of the past have failed, and the wounds have festered.

Every single Australian should evaluate the role they can play in the process. For some, it will be tough and may even involve major changes in behaviour. Others can try a kind word or understanding attitude. The task for those who can is facilitating change for each indigenous age group and demographic. Start by getting it right ASAP with the basic needs. If we follow the Maslow hierarchical model, the very young will be the easiest to help, because they have not been hurt too much... hopefully. Then each different age group will be at distinct stages struggling with the issues faced at their stage of development or demise.

It's a massive job with major hurdles to overcome. The first step is a universal change in thinking and a real universal ownership of the problem. Then, on to well-funded, direct, and compassionate intervention by well-informed trained people who want to help. This should be facilitated and backed by a majority of Australians, all willing to do what they can to truly welcome our indigenous people into the family—the classroom, the workplace, even the neighbourhood.

With that, however, indigenous people will need to transition to a forward-seeking solution based on forgiveness and a willingness to embrace what is best for an Australia that accepts, includes, recognises, and respects them.

There is, of course, a huge need for help, restitution, and change. But this cannot be in ignorance or denial of the damage that harshness and even unwise gifting has caused in the past.

Returning to the analogy, nowhere in the Parenting 101 manual does it say that you must put kids in charge. They need all the above with well-defined clear boundaries, wise guidance to keep them safe, and an environment that they trust enough to play safely in as they grow and develop. Without this parenting aspect, people just don't do well. (And again, it's not their fault!)

Back to the analogy. The ultimate aim of good parenting is to give responsibility and accountability. First Nation people must be the main players in shaping their own future. Once my kids came of age, there was no way they wanted me dictating terms to them anymore, but they know the door is always open, I am on their side, and I want what is best for them. They come to me for advice and know that if I think they are doing the wrong thing, they will hear from me. Hey, they give me advice too—I even listen.

I have said a lot, but my main message and first step is for both groups to adopt a new way of thinking about and processing what has occurred. These will then facilitate, enable, and stimulate what needs to occur next. It's a big ask, but not undoable.

There is nothing wrong with Australia Day marking and remembering the beginning of colonising Australia, but let's have another day to celebrate a real reconciliation based on universal honesty, respect, acceptance, forgiveness, and sincerity. We are moving in the right direction, but it has not happened yet.

If Australia can recognise and honour our First Nation people and their proud and ancient culture, incorporating it into a united, truly multicultural nation where all are valued, then we will have succeeded. An outside-the-box thought on this might be, 'The last thing we need is more division or separatism based on race.' This, I fear, is the direction our First Nation people are heading, because they have no faith or trust. This, because they simply don't feel the love. They don't feel accepted or they don't want to be accepted, and I can't really say I blame them.

An outside-the-box idea to help might include employing mainly First Nation people in the next-phase solution. So after the initial largely symbolic but essential inclusion in any republic or new constitution and flag, then the real work could begin. It is then that we set about subsidising and encouraging the training and employing of First Nation people to become their own solution. Teachers, hospital staff, police, firemen, rangers, counsellors, psychologists, lawyers, and more will then be proudly helping their own people.

Solutions that are intrinsically racist and separatist are not what are needed. Australia's coming of age, with a sensitive inclusive constitution making all Australians equal, should suffice. It does not offer revenge or payback but would ultimately benefit all. Here is another outside-the-box thought: how about free education (including tertiary) for First Nation people as, to quote a *crypto* term, 'proof of love'? The movement is already underway with a lot of genuine efforts being made to recognise and compensate where possible. It will never erase the memories or the damage—that will take time. And it can never turn back the clock. Australians must look forward together.

Chapter 6

Australia Day And Independence Day

Australia is a multicultural nation, and that includes all Australians. Australia Day is a celebration of this, in my view. Yes, it is the day the British landed. The start of the Australia we now all know and love. To my knowledge, the terrible things that have happened to our indigenous people did not actually start on this day. That came later and occurred over an extended period.

We as a nation regret the sins of our forefathers in this regard, and I believe there is now a strong movement in the right direction. We cannot change what has happened, but the stage is set for reconciliation and change. I believe there will soon be a great day that should be celebrated primarily by our indigenous people, but it is one that all Australians can join in.

It must be inclusive and reflect recognition, inclusiveness, understanding, forgiveness, and acceptance from all and encourage oneness as a nation, not division based on race (which is indeed racial prejudice). Solutions moving forward are in grave danger of causing more division if the focus is on payback, revenge, and other separatist notions.

Such a day has not yet come, but it might not be far away. My outside-the-box thought in this regard is 'Independence Day' as a day to mark Australia coming of age as a republic. Starting anew with a new constitution—one that truly recognises Australia's First Nation people as well as all other Australians. This day would recognise the background and heritage of all Australians and our nation. This, with the Queen's blessing—well, before she passes. It would also be an opportunity to address the many things that are not quite right and start anew in many regards.

We don't want two nations or two flags or two national anthems or a two-party adversarial government. We need one nation, one flag that reflects a new Australia and honors the heritage of all, one anthem that is inclusive and accepted by all.

We need a system of government which encourages support and respect for a democratically elected leader and government. Yes, there needs to be opposition and elections and different parties, but this business of opposing and knocking everything must stop. A democratically elected leader and government must have a mandate to achieve, over a period, with the cooperation of other players.

Ultimately, leaders should rightly be judged at the end of their term, democratically. Having a go is a part of being Australian. This must be allowed, encouraged, and embraced. I, for one, I am ashamed to see some of the behaviors of our leaders in the public eye.

Chapter 7

Superannuation And Retirement

From the outset, I will put to you an outside-the-box concept on this. In my view, anyone who has worked and paid tax should be entitled to a retirement income, with the minimum an adequate pension.

Other countries do it; why can't we? Well, simply put, in Australia, the government clearly got it wrong. They devised a superannuation system which was supposed to achieve self-funded retirement for most people. It has not and will not.

To devise a system that allows and encourages tax minimization then expect people to not fully exploit and take full advantage of legal avenues is puerile. It does not consider human nature.

Further, to outline, the amounts you may have invested in your family home and in the bank to qualify for the pension is simply going to be adhered to. The lucky ones will spend their superannuation money on their home, world trip, new boat or car, etc. so that they qualify for the pension to some extent. Only the very fortunate or wealthy will be self-funded retirees.

In Australia, there is a massive amount of the public purse tied up in superannuation, and the government is scratching its head, trying to work out how to fix the problem it created. Short of confiscating most of it and starting again, they will change the rules over time to partially address their problem.

Simply put, you need about four or five hundred thousand in super to earn the equivalent of the pension. Most people don't have that much. Their latest effort seems to inhibit and restrict catch-up payments as well. Those who want to put more into super during their final working years, when they can finally afford to, are limited and cannot 'tax effectively'. Oh, I know, that would decrease tax revenue a little, but surely the trade-off would be worth it.

It would make more sense to encourage the deposit of extra funds to super up to the limit, as well as impose a full tax on the withdrawal of these contributions, unless for approved purposes, e.g. medical costs or to pay off a modest family home, etc. Many pay off the mortgage first, then try to top up their super but are restricted.

Ultimately, however, in my view, the government will need to take out a percentage of everyone's wage (no exceptions) to fund retirement. Then they can pay everyone who qualifies an adequate pension. This will mean the more you earn, the more you pay. Any extra you save for a more comfortable retirement might be a matter of choice, not tax-deductible, and without the fear of Big Brother penalizing you for being successful. Yes, that's right: earn more and pay more, but no more poor pensioners. Everyone will be in the same boat. The savings on administration and compliance would be enormous.

The transition to such a system would be very difficult, but not impossible. Tax records clearly show gross earnings over time. Once the percentage is worked out, this would be, like most taxes, a sliding scale and the calculation reasonably straightforward.

The process would certainly see winners and losers initially, but the result would be a system that benefits all Australians.

Yes, for it to work, the government would virtually need to take control or, dare I say, confiscate most supers. Those who have saved very well for their retirement would need to be recognized and rewarded. It would be a hard one to sell indeed. One consolation would be the knowledge that it would create a fairer Australia for our children. Certainly outside-the-box thinking.

To achieve such brave, radical initiatives, leadership and principles that are more than socialistic or capitalistic are needed. We need to be futuristic and realistic, get outside the box, and finally consider all aspects of our human nature.

Just as a reminder, we can be

- kind, generous, understanding, forgiving, gracious, caring, considerate, unselfish, public-minded, fair, reasonable, and more; or
- unkind, selfish, self-centered, unforgiving, uncaring, inconsiderate, selfish, greedy, ruthless, cruel, corrupt, unfair, unreasonable, and more.

Neither side is going away soon, so public programs and initiatives must consider the best and the worst of human nature to be effective and successful over time.

Chapter 8

Health Insurance

The outside-the-box thought here is a public health service funded by a percentage of income. This could work a lot better than the current system.

Private health insurance is becoming more expensive and is struggling to compete with the public system. The actual cost to those who are privately insured now would likely go down, and the cost to those who are not privately insured might increase slightly. But the result would be an easily administered system where the amount you pay is proportional to the amount you earn for everyone. No loopholes. No opting out. With that, however, don't make the same mistake of ignoring human nature and greed. Clear controls, guidelines, and clinical indicators for all services and procedures would need to be developed, auditable, and enforceable. No, you cannot have expensive special procedures electively. The culture of presenting at the emergency department for non-urgent issues to save money would diminish. The advent of well-located large super clinics is already partially addressing this problem.

Most private hospitals would need to adopt the public system, though some, I am sure, might choose to cater to those who choose to continue outside the system despite the unavoidable compulsory contribution into the public system.

Chapter 9

Employment Ethics

Now that unions have less involvement and jobs are scarcer, individuals are unlikely to even say 'Boo!' when they are treated unfairly or even illegally. It's a small world now, and in many arenas, everyone knows everyone, so it does not pay to squeak, let alone be a whistle-blower.

I have experienced this first-hand and will share here just as an example.

I have missed out on work that went to non-Australian citizens without workers' visas. On one occasion, the same company offered me work as a contractor. When I voiced that I cannot and prefer a casual employment contract (which would include worker's comp, super, payroll tax, and insurance), I was told that I would be providing equipment, so I could be a contractor. To my surprise, the 'equipment' was boots and a hard hat (PPE). On this occasion, the job went to an

Australian that lived in Vietnam who was more flexible. I did inform the Department of Immigration and the tax office but heard nothing back from them. Subsequently, I was blacklisted by this company, who also put the word out that I was a troublemaker when they were referee-called as an ex-employer. With no union representation for this sector of the workforce, it would have been more advisable to say nothing.

While it is true that some unions have at times gone too far, I believe that all workers need to be protected and represented. The worst aspects of human nature will always emerge on the part of some employers and employees if there are no checks and balances.

This is, perhaps, another thing that could be revisited in our new constitution on 'Independence Day': clear universal guidelines and enforceable laws developed to moderate and control the employment arena.

This combined with human nature proof solutions, that reward employers for paying wages rather than penalizing, would benefit. Make paying wages more attractive than other expenditure and removing payroll tax could be considered.

Chapter 10

Buying A Home

I have no problem with mums and dads getting ahead with a negatively geared property. It's a bit of an Australian tradition. God knows, we don't have many, and it provides rental properties. I do, however, have big problems with international non-citizens competing with my kids for a home.

I have touched on foreign ownership. It's time to reverse it. Outside-the-box thought: any land, businesses, or homes; that are predominantly foreign owned; could perhaps, revert to something like a thirty-year lease. This type of significant move, only becomes palatable under the umbrella of 'Independence Day', when we 'press reset', form a republic, write a new constitution and fix this mess.

Chapter 11

Education

Education is fundamentally important to every aspect of our lives. Without diminishing the importance of the basic—reading, writing, arithmetic, and the sciences—a lot more is needed.

The outside-the-box concept here is to make education a lot more inclusive. With knowledge and preparation, future generations will be better-equipped to cope with and solve a lot of the issues we are struggling with today.

For example, we have talked about indigenous issues.

I recently went through a process of mandatory learning as a public servant in the health arena in Western Australia. It struck me that they handled indigenous issues very well. This kind of education should be a part of every school curriculum. The subject and theme to start in grade one, then progress and develop right through to graduation. In addition to a compulsory subject at all schools, a further e-learning course could be developed along the same lines for all Australians. Only through awareness, education, and knowledge will all be better equipped to cope. Changed hearts and minds come from education, knowledge, and understanding, not ignorance.

Parenting is probably the most important undertaking any of us will attempt in this lifetime. Sadly, this knowledge is not hereditary, nor is it necessarily taught by example in the home. It is an often-daunting task, and one too many so readily ridicule their parents' failings. So begins the cycle of opposites where one takes an opposing view to their parents.

Even worse is the case where virtually no parenting has been done sometimes for generations, to produce totally antisocial tendencies.

Yes, I am suggesting parenting classes in the school system. The framework is already there. Some parenting teaching principles hold true across the board, and some do not. A healthy knowledge of each, made relevant in the context of historical trends and cultural and religious influences, would give understanding to students.

Enhance the relevance of parenting to balanced development. With that, it would also facilitate an environment where students who are victim to such various pressures might, with understanding, seek the help or guidance they may need.

Another potentially harmful trend which might benefit from education is the use, misuse, and influence of social media. Children are bombarded from an early age and, whether we like it or not, are heavily influenced.

The effects on many aspects of decision-making and choices are shaped online. One I have noticed, as an example, is the tendency of many young people to want or need the best of everything first up, from clothing to first car and first home. This encourages early debt that can be crippling. The list goes on: road use or drug and alcohol abuse come to mind.

The outside-the-box principle here is, through education and understanding, many of our biggest problems today could be mitigated.

Oh yes. I think I mentioned free tertiary education for First Nation people. It's the least we can do.

Chapter 12

Respecting Sexual Preferences

It's been interesting to watch the same-sex marriage issue unfold. I see everyone embracing the acceptance of the concept, but I do ponder a little on deeper thoughts. Surely, these people should have recognition so that they can live meaningful lives, protected by law and secure in their relationships. Yes, they exist, and they have a place in society and the right to live without persecution or fear. There is, however, a difference between accepting, tolerating, even facilitating, and encouraging or even promoting.

The reality is, a substantial portion of the population have interpersonal and sexual preferences that differ. It is right that this be acknowledged and that the rights, freedoms, and preferences of all be respected. This group is, by nature, outgoing—even flamboyant—so while I respect the right of all to be recognised in legal marriage, this, in my view, marks a point where society must review which interpersonal behaviours are suitable for public viewing. Personally, I like to see a male and female kissing. It seems quite natural to me. In the same way, I am sure, same-sex couples see it as their right to also kiss in public, on TV, etc. Well, this is where we need to reassess. For example, I (like many) find it upsetting to see two men kissing. The answer is quite simple, really. We need to respect each other's preferences and perhaps agree on what level of physical interaction is appropriate for general viewing. It may sound harsh and draconian, but we already, as a society, say no to sexually explicit acts on TV. This is a simple progression of the same concept. The various ways we make, and express love is best kept out of the public eye. Influences on the young and innocent in this regard should be provided and filtered by family and friends. Now that the doors are open, we as a society need to reassess the boundaries in a considerate, sensitive, mature manner. Unfortunately, the thinking of some in this arena is, 'We have arrived. They can't stop us now. Where to from here?'

The gay Mardi Gras parade, for example, was to promote awareness and recognition of same-sex relationships and transgender individuals. This, has been accomplished, so now the gay and lesbian Mardi Gras is really just a great excuse for a huge televised public celebration/party.

The outside-the-box thought here is, now the LGBTI community is mainstream, they could consider a bit of self-regulation, to show that they deserve the trust and recognition the majority have lent them. I dare say, when given a place at the table, behavioural etiquette should be considered.

The mechanics of making love, let's say, are various and need to stay behind closed doors in a civilised, inclusive, respectful, modern society.

The reality is, history shows, majority rule often gets it wrong. We in this age are pushing the boundaries at every turn. Whether we like to admit it or not, in the absence of self-regulation, it is our leaders who should moderate the excesses of our human nature.

That's why we have diverse leaders and representation in parliament—I hope!

Chapter 13

Gender Issues

Wow, what a diverse, sensitive, individual, emotive, and important but basic, dangerous, and problematic arena. Influenced by tradition, religion, geography, politics, sexuality, and importantly, personal experience, these are exciting, troubling times. I must be crazy to attempt it.

My outside-the-box concept on this one is an attempt to be sensible, unbiased, honest, kind, and gracious but brave enough to state the facts. A main hurdle is that the vast majority of us clearly must identify with one of the two camps, so making it more difficult for anyone to truly remain neutral, objective, unbiased, and dare I say, logical and accepting.

Grace, by definition, is undeserved favor.

'A friend is one to whom one may pour out the contents of one's heart, chaff and grain together, knowing that gentle hands will take and sift it,

keep what is worth keeping, and with a breath of kindness, blow the rest away' (George Eliot).

With this in mind, let's continue the discussion with *friendly grace*.

There is absolutely no doubt that the fairer sex has had it rough, in many respects, for far too long in so many ways that there is no need to rehash them here—men in power abusing their position to take advantage of women being the big one. Following on from the obvious and the horrible, however, is a huge grey area of what is acceptable from both sides.

Remembering that this is outside-the-box thinking by definition, I would like to explore a few of the less obvious aspects. Let us get back to basics: in general, men have desires and urges that are entirely different to those of women. These affect behaviours in many ways. The outcomes are largely dependent on the conditioning offered by parenting, friends, culture, religion, education, and peer group pressure. The list goes on and on. The simple fact of the matter is that the accepted popular norm is a baseline that sweeps most in the same direction. With that, however, there will be variations of unacceptable behaviors which would be seen by the majority to be unacceptable. These punishable deviations break the law and are caused by individuals who knowingly, recklessly, or plain stupidly push the boundaries too far. There are also those who are perhaps not too smart, well-parented, or whatever who push the boundaries a little in what I would call a normal variation. These concern me. We are not all rocket scientists, you know.

It is, a very intimidating, confusing, and frustrating arena for many. I am perhaps fairly normal, brought up in a sound Christian home, and well educated, but I assure you, this whole area still amazes me. I had a rule which helped me cope. It should perhaps be considered. Even though, quite naturally, I thought I was a devastatingly handsome young man (stop it!), I would never approach a member of the fairer sex unless she made the first move. I assure you, it did not need to be much of a move—a look or a smile is enough. Simple, really, but some guys never get it, and unfortunately some girls abuse it.

Now out of this waffle, there emerges some vitally significant issues. The bar has been raised, if you like; the goalposts have moved. What was considered by the majority to be acceptable has changed and will continue to change. With this change comes a need to reassess how 'the game is played.

If you go back in thirty- or even twenty-year leaps, you will observe marked differences in all sorts of things. It was not that long ago that almost everyone smoked almost everywhere. To what extent should we go back in time and gather evidence and prosecute past behaviours using today's standards? Extreme care is needed to navigate through this. There is currently a lot of enthusiasm with women coming forward. Many have suffered horrifically, but I fear some may be on the bandwagon, so caution is needed. Reputations can be ruined and lives destroyed. We must avoid trial by media.

I, like many, am a bit old school, I guess. I like girls to be girls and boys to be boys. I delight in playing the game by traditional rules. One where women are proud to be women, embracing their gifts. And likewise, one where men are proud to be men, treating all women with respect—hopefully with a special one as *'princess for life'*.

Whoops, I just woke from a dream. Sorry, where was I? Back to reality. Some women now play football, do not want a door opened for them, and are insulted rather than flattered when their beauty is recognised by a man. Now we hear that some don't like being referred to as *mankind*, *women*, or *female* because these terms contain the word *male* and so imply male domination. The word *ridiculous* springs to mind but may not be allowed, because if spelt phonetically, it may be inappropriate. Hmm! Not my cup of tea at all. Better to move on to a safer topic.

Before I do, however, and because this work is titled *Outside the Box*, I would like to share further outside-the-box observations.

Next, you may laugh, cry, scream, or just scratch your head. We are leaving the box!

Far too many female presenters and guests on TV and other media seem to be adopting what could be described as a nasal monotone way of speaking. The result is a deeper-sounding voice that is in no way feminine. Now if this is the intention, then fine; but half the time, it is the result of someone speaking very fast. The outcome is 'speaking at you' rather than 'speaking to you'. The problem is that, at best, it actually sends a message like, 'I don't care what you think. I have no time for you. I really don't want to be talking to you. It is not important to be pleasant right now.' At worst it sends a message like, 'I am angry with you. I simply don't like you. I am better than you. I am wasting my time talking to you.' Now admittedly, some men are doing it too, but not as much. We would not get away with it very often anyway. Many men, however, will sound like this when they are angry or fed up.

Now, I am certain that a lot of you are spitting chips at me right now. Take a moment and listen. This trend exists. It is not necessarily intentional, but it is certainly not desirable and it diminishes you.

I think most can agree there is nothing wrong with women looking attractive. There is also nothing wrong with sounding attractive. Indeed, in direct interpersonal interactions, most people speak respectfully to each other unless the intention is to not be nice. My main point is that if you are doing this in the public eye and cannot control the way you sound, you may be in the wrong job.

You may also be affecting ratings. I, for one, change channels every time because I can.

Since I am on a roll, I will also tackle an age-old favorite. In this age of equality, regardless of gender, sexual orientation, or time of the month, it is no longer OK to be in a bitchy mood. We all need to act and interact in a civil, polite, considerate, and I dare say, pleasant—even professional—manner. I have worked in almost every type of workplace, from hospitals to workshops, farms, factories, offices, and more, and in many countries. With this authority, in my view, the most admirable interpersonal environment in this regard that I have worked in is the offshore OGP (oil gas producer) arena. Suboptimal behaviours are simply not tolerated at all.

Outside-the-box thought: perhaps in this brave new equal rights arena, hopefully, we might well see less 'angry and moody' happening. Hey what happened to a safer topic?

Chapter 14

'Me Too'

I am totally supportive of this movement, which is directed primarily at respecting a woman's right to be respected. Every situation, including the workplace, must be free from sexual harassment and gender-based mistreatment. This has raised many relevant conversations which I have no intention of rehashing here.

The outside-the-box thought I would raise in this context could be labeled 'Male Me Too' and is solely based on my own personal life. I submit this as examples of just one person's life experience wondering, Am I Robinson Crusoe, or is this another widespread, unaddressed problem?

I suggest that it could often be as difficult for a male to come forward with a complaint as it is for a female. I won't even mention being caned by a nun in first grade for hugging Rosemary Clifton. We will keep this more current.

In a female-dominated workplace, I found myself tormented by a moody, grumpy, unreasonable red-headed female work colleague. Apart from being difficult—most of the time, mainly towards male staff—she was particularly bad. Let's say, 'periodically'. This built up over time. I stupidly said nothing. One day, I finally cracked and said to her, 'You are just being bitchy.' She immediately broke down in tears, running to the female supervisor and saying I had called her a bitch and she wanted to go home and not work with me. HR was called in—more females—and I was severely reprimanded, not listened to, and told to submit a written report. To cut a long story short, it did not end well for me because I used the word *bitch*. The redhead got worse, and I resigned.

On another occasion, I was one of two males in a lecture room setting where a drop-dead gorgeous female was giving a talk to the largely female group. At one stage during the talk, she made a joke which I, in fact, enjoyed and laughed at, but it was totally inappropriate. During the context of her talk, she used the words *six inches* then paused; and looking directly at me, she held her index finger and thumb up and said, 'And, guys, this is three inches, not six inches.' The entire room erupted in raucous laughter—including me. With that, however, clearly she had engaged in a sexual gender joke. The point here is that though I appreciated the wit, it was very wrong. I don't think even the most handsome guy would get away with cracking a joke about small boobs in a room full of men with only two women in the room.

On another occasion, a very attractive female supervisor of mine was quite seductive towards me at a Christmas party even though my wife was present. This caused quite a problem at home for me.

On another occasion, I was used by a woman to get her pregnant because her best friend had fallen pregnant. Of course, I did not complain at the time because I was smitten by her, but I certainly paid the price many times over, to say the least.

I, like most, have other stories that would make hair grow on your teeth, but unlike many, I think that the real strength lies in the wisdom of silence to protect loved ones.

'Keep what is worth keeping, and with a breath of kindness, blow the rest away.'

In a nutshell: Many people, male and female, need to correct bad behaviours, both overt and subtle. Many cultures do not tolerate displays of anger, moodiness, or sexual innuendo. Some have women covered up, and some, on display. Some have men out of control; some have women out of control. Next, I guess we will have gays out of control. One thing is certain: things are changing.

The outside-the-box principle here is, no matter the sex or sexual orientation, it's is no longer OK to have a bad behavior day, and it has never been ok to 'poke with a stick'.

Chapter 15

The Church

The church has come under a lot of scrutiny lately, to do with child abuse and the frustrated sexual tendencies of the clergy—and quite rightly so. The Royal Commission names celibacy as one of the root causes. Talk about stating the obvious. I have an outside-the-box thought I would like to throw into the mix based on a personal life experience.

As a young boy, it was thought that I was troubled. Now, in fact, this came about because of what one might call enthusiastic sibling rivalry. Fairly common, even normal, interactions found me outnumbered by my sisters and isolated from my dad to a point where I felt isolated, unloved, and lonely, then became withdrawn, morose, and angry.

Well, the solution was clear to all. I had to be encouraged to join the priesthood. Make no mistake, this was real pressure. You may well laugh, but especially in a strong Roman Catholic arena, if you were troubled—especially in conjunction with interpersonal difficulties with the fairer sex—you were pushed into the priesthood.

Now it needs to be said, I am heterosexual. With that, however, we all know that . . . let's say, 'different' . . . sexual preferences and tendencies do exist. They always have existed. Only recently has society accepted this.

The outside-the-box thought here: it is quite possible that a disproportionate number of individuals with frustrated or confused tendencies may have, through the years, been pushed by society into the priesthood as a solution.

Think about it! What options, for example, did a homosexual have? Society had not tolerated or recognised homosexuality yet, so you were in for an unhappy life to say the least. On the other hand, becoming a priest was the pinnacle of achievement and most respected. This dilemma faced unknowingly could be one of the factors that influenced choices made by some.

This tendency would be more likely in the past than now, perhaps, but the legacy we have now certainly seems to indicate something has gone seriously wrong.

Chapter 16

Islam Today

Recently we had a national census where we had to tick the boxes.

Under Christian, there were quite a few choices. The different sects of Christianity have identified with like-minded individuals proudly. They are each no less Christian for this, but can comfortably and safely practice their religion with others who have similar beliefs and preferences. Importantly, however, outsiders have a pretty good idea of where they stand on most issues.

An outside-the-box thought here is that for Islam, there was only one box to tick. It said *Muslim*. Could this be the fundamental error of Islam today? Clearly, there is a need for Muslims to identify with like-minded Muslims in an unambiguous, clear, open way. Then they can freely and proudly practise their religion with like-minded individuals.

Importantly, on the world stage today, it can no longer be tolerated for such a diverse group to walk under the same banner. They do only out of fear of persecution from within Islam—perhaps by the very ones they want to distance themselves from. Extreme Islam is telling moderate, tolerant, generally harmless Islam that they will not condone division in Islam. Hard to argue within their culture, but most Muslims are delightful people who try hard to assimilate and fit into the multicultural, diverse, respectful, and tolerant modern mindset.

With the current worldwide turmoil, it would even be reasonable for governments to insist that all religions, including Islam, should make a basic statement of beliefs on intentions.

Simple, really: with the assistance of religious leaders (or not), there needs to be a categorization process. And yes, it needs to be compulsory, a swearing on your holy book. Identify with like-minded individuals for the good of all concerned. Once there is a framework, then both individuals and governments can start the process of administering appropriately, within the framework, and understanding the framework around which they are prepared to operate.

To assist in the process, different questions could arise to clarify where individuals stand. And to help confirmation, again people could tick the box of their preferred response... This would be a tool to help individuals in the process of finding where they best fit into the framework as well as to have something tangible in the vetting process around immigration, etc.

The range of questions is huge, from 'Do you agree with the methods of ISIS? Is it OK to behead people to advance the cause?' etc., to 'Do you believe men and women have an equal right to education?' Even 'Would you allow a female headmistress of a school to publicly award your son a merit award or prefer to just pass on it because of your beliefs?'

Once a framework is established, then the process is less nebulous and policy can be formulated. It may turn out that distinct groups are deemed unsuitable or incompatible with certain societies or countries. This all under oath, with one hand on the appropriate holy book, in writing signed and witnessed to minimise false declarations. The extremist would be unlikely to be willing to lie before their god.

This would also mean that, for example, Australia would need to rewrite the constitution to include and exclude different things. For example, bigamy could be, might be against the law. Women's rights could be documented as a minimum standard behaviour. Specified undesirable, harmful, or antisocial features could even be named.

The do-gooder, accept-all, and open-door policies are now problematic. *Damaging* does not even begin to describe the harm that complacency in this matter will bring. Look daily at the current examples of what can happen in this matter. The world is an ever-smaller place, and time is precious.

Chapter 17

Taking Life

"Thou shalt not kill." Straight out of the Bible, but like many things, it seems open to interpretation.

A modern version of this might be, 'Thou shalt not kill unless necessary, convenient, and socially acceptable.' How far do we logically take this? During a time of war, in self-defense, or administering control of law are the obvious examples where there may be little choice in the matter.

Can we even agree on when there is life? Most agree that life ends when the heart stops. Is it perhaps reasonable therefore, to agree life begins when the heart starts?

What about when there is a choice? Capital punishment, termination of pregnancy, and euthanasia are the big ones in this arena.

Capital punishment is an interesting one. The trend is away from capital punishment. It is seen as barbaric and unnecessary even when it appears justified. It is almost always non-consensual, and mistakes can happen.

In my view, euthanasia in the case of suffering, dying people may not be seen as barbaric in any way. It is defining the quality and quantity of life when medically justified and is totally consensual. We condone it for our pets but not for other members of our family. These people have had a full life and have the right of choice.

Termination of pregnancy is, for some reason, widely accepted. The arguments in favor start with rape and fetal abnormalities, but these represent a relatively small portion. Most terminations are simply unwanted pregnancies and involve choice. Unlike capital punishment, the victim is totally innocent; and unlike euthanasia, it is always non-consensual. If un-interfered with, these silent, defenseless people would develop normally into contributing members of the community. Being small only means there is not much evidence and disposal is easy. The choice, if made, to not have sex or to use contraception seems a lot more socially acceptable to me. This may, however, cause minor inconvenience at times.

Worthy of note at this point, is the fact that adoption has become extremely difficult, even prohibitive. There are many wonderful, loving couples (including LGBTI) who would gladly adopt a child if they could. This choice should not be classified as outside-the-box and needs to be part of a sensitive, inclusive future.

The outside-the-box thought on this is, history will judge this practice in the same way as it judged slavery, the Holocaust, invading less-developed countries, burning witches at the stake, or the Spanish Inquisition—i.e. 'It was widely accepted by many and legal for a time!' I am ashamed to say that I played a part in this as a young man. The choice to marry, I can say with hindsight, would most likely have been a good one. But because we were young, it seemed the sensible choice to terminate the pregnancy. The reality is that it was the easy choice and one I, like many, deeply regret. This act ruined a beautiful relationship, and the child had no choice.

The factors effecting a decision to take life appear to be choice, convenience, justice, disposal, public opinion, consent and defining life.

The latter two raising the most significant, poignant, helpful of questions. Was there informed consent to begin or end the life? Does the accepted definition of life, leave room to remedy the dilemma's especially of consent, convenience and choice?

Chapter 18

Crypto

Many people still have a poor understanding of what crypto is. If you believe the future is digital, computer- and Internet-based, then it is time to for you to consider learning about crypto.

In a nutshell, the concept might be described as an Internet-based global digitizing of transactions that does not rely on banks as middlemen and will be free from manipulation and control. The enormous number of platforms and controls, to make this secure, convenient, and acceptable to all stakeholders are being developed at a staggering pace. Like any major change or development or new technological era, the process will take time, and it will evolve over time into something we have not yet perhaps dreamt of.

Remember that not so long ago, movies were discovered. We went to the cinema, then to our homes, Beta, and VHS, then discs. Now we can live-stream to many devices. I don't think this was foreseen when Super 8 came out. Beta did not take off. But there were still a lot of winners along the way.

One thing, however, was certain. Movies as well as computers, phones, and the Internet are here to stay.

Crypto, is here to stay, so get on board and start learning about it. Already there is a lot to learn. Then take a portion of your worth that you are willing to lose, make some careful, initially small speculative investments in crypto and start the learning process. I personally have been on a journey with an advisory service for many years. I don't mind paying for their guidance and tuition.

To introduce you to a crypto term, I will even 'show some love', and give them a plug. Some, in my view, are doing an excellent job in this arena. They offer some services for free. Some cost a little, and some cost more. As with most things, you basically get what you pay for. To have a look and spend a little on your education in this regard is, in my view, wise.

Some of us remember when computers took off. They are now vitally essential.

Chapter 19

Religion

Wow, what am I doing? Isn't this one of those things you just don't talk about?

Well, this is the problem: we need to talk about this and even address the matter in our new constitution. The past is full of often-terrible things done in the name of religion. We cannot just accept all comers without scrutiny. If a new religion emerges, it must self-define in simple terms the fundamentals, goals, rules, and intentions. Likewise, for old established religions, it may no longer be acceptable to all walk under the same banner. (See chapter 16, 'Islam Today'.)

Then modern society is informed and prepared to accept or reject it. The constitution could use concepts like

- Persons may not freely and openly propose to harm, disadvantage, or mislead the innocent.
- Persons may not use their position to use or abuse the innocent.
- Persons with knowledge of unlawful or harmful acts or intentions towards the innocent, no matter how this knowledge is gained, must use this knowledge to improve outcomes for the innocent.
- Persons may not, knowingly or recklessly, condone or allow unlawful acts or behaviors in the name of religion.

Obviously, I am not a lawyer, and the above is just an attempt to flavor and encourage outside-the-box thinking in this arena.

Chapter 20

Defining Australian

This is so important and so neglected. It's great to be multicultural, but now that we are of age, it is time to define ourselves in a sensitive, inclusive constitution. With that, however, it is important to outline guidelines practical and behavioural—to draw the line, if you like, so that people know what is and is not expected from all who call themselves Australian in our proud nation.

For example, the 'riotous' behaviours that are daily occurrences in some parts of the world . . . and seen on media, on the news, etc., and include, large unruly large groups roaming the streets. —burning flags chanting, shouting, and violence marking . . . the 'way they roll.' While common in the Middle East, some parts of Asia, Africa, and indeed, other countries, it is not common place in Australia . . . It's simply not the way 'we roll.' We don't like it, and most Australians are horrified by it. Even our First Nation People, who have been much maligned over the years, generally have the pride, dignity, and respect for themselves and this country to not stoop to these barbaric behaviours.

This, is why the recent riotous behaviours displayed by a small number of Sudanese youth in Melbourne, has received such public condemnation. It's not, that it is such a huge group, but more that it is reminiscent, perhaps, of what is seen in their homeland. It's not what most want to see in Australia. We need to draw the line, if you like, so that people know what is, and is not expected in our proud nation from all who call themselves Australian, in our proud nation.

Defining what is acceptable and what is not acceptable is not discriminatory—it is considerate. To get back to the parenting analogy, if you define the boundaries, kids are better off. And they are less inclined to push till they cross the line. They already know where it is.

We can be multicultural as we have always been, but there is nothing wrong with being proud to be Australian as well. All Australians need to accept a high standard of decency, tolerance, and respect for a constitution that is yet to be written—one that protects the right of all creeds and groups, but forbids any one group to force others into adopting their particular belief, dietary or dress restrictions, and conditions. If you don't want to eat certain food or if you want to wear certain clothing, that's your prerogative. With that, however, if you go into Australian courts or schools, then you need to follow the traditional dress codes of that institution and have no right to break our rules. If it's a school, then you had better find another school. If it's our courts, then you have no choice. And if you don't like all this, the perhaps you are in the wrong country.

The outside-the-box thought here is that non-citizens and new Australians could remain under scrutiny for a period. If you take up any job, even if you are eminently qualified, you will willingly submit to a probationary period. This is a period during which you had better be on your best behaviour or you are out. Now, if with fair warning, during your probationary period, you still breach the conditions of your contract, it is usually safe to say you might be in the wrong place.

The outside-the-box thought on this is that the treasured job of being Australian is no different.

Again, a recent suggestion that a high level of English be essential is a not solution. A basic level of English and the ability to communicate are helpful, will naturally occur over time, and should be facilitated.

Certain crimes and behaviours during a probationary period could perhaps be rewarded (by the courts) with a free one-way ticket back to wherever you came from.

Epilogue

Here are a few more thoughts to encourage outside-the-box thinking:

PROSTITUTION

The oldest profession—it's biblical, consensual, and should be legal and taxed and controlled like any other essential service industry.

REFUGEES

Would it be possible, I wonder, to somehow offer a temporary safe haven in a closed town where they would certainly be better off, looked after, and even allowed to earn their keep to a certain extent till they can return to their country of origin safely?

WATER

This is not even outside the box. It's bloody obvious and has been thought of before. Australia is huge and a lot of it only lacks water and power. We have the largest freshwater supply in the southern hemisphere, Lake Argyle. I picture a massive black plastic pipeline—hopefully made out of recycled plastics. Yes, a canal system might be easier, but it would perhaps waste too much water.

The country needs this. It has been discussed before, and nothing has happened. Why?

Some downhill sections could perhaps make power. I'm not sure. Perhaps it would heat the water so much it self-pressurises. How about a huge mobile plastic-extruder truck driving through the desert spitting pipe out the back? Hmm . . . I like that one! New towns springing up, populated by refugees happily working in our factories, all straight from Germany, who happily helped finance it. Hmm . . . there's a thought.

NATIONAL BROADBAND NETWORK (NBN)

Great idea, but the real future in communications seems to lean towards wireless technologies. Optional fibre to schools, business, and some individuals who really need it is perhaps justified.

An outside-the-box thought on this is that money spent on fibre to transmission towers and satellites might be more beneficial in the long term. Technology is rolling on and will not go backwards. G5 is rolling out as we speak. G10 will be amazing. The race into the future needs to be dynamic enough to change direction when indicated. Personally, I use Internet to my phone and tether other devices to it. This is adequate for me now and will only get faster. Well under $50 per month gives me all my local calls, quite a lot of international calls, and all the Internet I need wherever I am. I don't even have a landline.

I think you get the idea.

Think about it, talk about it, and if you want, please share your thoughts by following us on twitter. (e.g. #OTB1, = Outside-the-Box Chapter 1)

Through the web site www.outsidetheboxthinking.com.au The author will consider: reader submissions, requests for respectful interview and discussion or interaction from interested parties or media, only upon application through the website 'CONTACT THE AUTHOR' page.

About The Website

- www.outsidetheboxthinking.com.au
- The website will include the 1000word free preview.
- The website will facilitate the ordering, payment for and delivery of hardcover, paperback or digital versions of this book. 'Outside-the-box, A Wind of Change'
- Reader participation encouraged on 'twitter' and interaction will be facilitated and strictly monitored on the website by the author.
- The author reserves the right to reject all or part of any post.
- The website will have a 'JOIN THE MAILING LIST' section. That means, if a viewer is interested in joining the mailing list or would want to opt-in on getting updates from the author, he or she will just need to fill out the form on this section and click on the button. Once done, an email will be

sent to the author, and that email message will consist of the information that was filled out by the viewer.

- The website will also have a 'CONTACT THE AUTHOR' page where interested parties can contact the author by filling out the form. Once they click on SUBMIT or SEND, an email will then be sent to authors email address.

About The Author

Outside the Box

A Wind of Change

The author, Pietro Barbara, is sixty-three years of age. Married twice, he has four kids, and is currently engaged. He is a second-generation Australian and widely travelled.

His work history is diverse, including careers in hospital paramedics, offshore oil and gas engineering, industrial and medical radiation work, mechanical/ hydraulics/ROV piloting, hospitality, small business ownership, wholesale distributing, importing and sales, rota-moulding, and more.

He has several tertiary qualifications, including a diploma in applied science, a postgraduate diploma in aquiculture, a 3.4U

CSWIP Underwater Inspection Controller certificate, a NEBOSH International General Certificate in Health Safety and Environment, front-line management, financial accounting, small business management, plastic fabricating, and more.

Index

A

adoption 56

Australia 1-4, 7-14, 16, 18-21, 23-4, 26-8, 54, 66

Australia Day 20, 23

Australian family 15-17

Australians 2, 15-16, 18-19, 21-4, 62-4

B

behaviour 10, 18, 39, 42-3, 46, 49, 54, 62-4

C

capital punishment 55-6

categorization 53

change 2-3, 9-10, 12-13, 15, 18-19, 23, 36, 43, 58

child abuse 50

Christianity 52

church xi-xii, 50

climate change 12-13

coming of age 9, 21, 24, 62

company tax 3

constitution 8, 10, 21, 24, 33-4, 54, 60, 62-3

crypto 21, 58-9

E

education 21, 35-7

English 64

euthanasia 55-6

F

First Nation People 15-16, 20-1, 24, 37, 62

flag 10, 21, 24, 62

foreign ownership 3, 8, 34

G

Gender Issues 41

Grace 41

H

harassment 47

hierarchy of needs 16, 19

homosexuals 39, 51, 56

human nature 3-5, 26, 28-30, 33, 40

I

Independence Day 8-9, 23-4, 33-4

indigenous people 10, 15-19, 23, 35

infants 16

Internet 58-9, 67

Islam 52-3, 60

M

'Me Too' movement 47

Melbourne 63

mood 46

Muslims 52-3

N

nasal monotone 45

NATIONAL BROADBAND NETWORK (NBN) 66

non-citizens 3, 34, 64

nuclear power 6-7, 13-14

O

opposition 3, 10, 12, 24

outside-the-box thoughts 4, 21, 24, 26, 28, 30, 34-5, 37, 41, 44, 46-7, 49, 51-2, 57, 61, 64-5, 67, 69

P

parenting 17, 20, 36, 63

pension 26-8

priesthood 50-1

property 34

PROSTITUTION 65

R

refugees 65-6

religion 52-3, 60-1

retirement 26-8

S

same-sex relationships 38-9

sexual preferences 38, 51

steel 6-7, 13

Sudanese youth 63

superannuation 3, 26-8, 59

T

tax 3-4, 8, 26-8, 32-3, 65

termination of pregnancy 55-7

Third World countries 1

two-party political system 3, 10, 12, 24

U

unions 32-3

W

water 7, 66

women's rights 54

'MY THOUGHTS'

'MY THOUGHTS'

'MY THOUGHTS'

'MY THOUGHTS'

'MY THOUGHTS'

www.ingramcontent.com/pod-product-compliance
Lightning Source LLC
Chambersburg PA
CBHW030909180526
45163CB00004B/1770